COMPASSION FATIGUE
IN THE FUNERAL PROFESSION

25 EVIDENCE-BASED STRATEGIES
TO MITIGATE FUNERAL CARE FATIGUE

INTERNATIONAL GRIEF INSTITUTE, LLC
www.InternationalGriefInstitute.com

Compassion Fatigue in the Funeral Profession – 1st ed.
Lynda Cheldelin Fell
International Grief Institute, LLC
www.InternationalGriefInstitute.com

Cover Design by AlyBlue Media, LLC
Interior Design by AlyBlue Media LLC
Published by AlyBlue Media, LLC
Copyright © 2022 by AlyBlue Media All rights reserved. No part of this publication may be reproduced, distributed or transmitted in any form or by any means, without prior written permission of the publisher.

AlyBlue Media, LLC
www.AlyBlueMedia.com
ISBN: 978-1-950712-51-9

This book is designed to provide informative narrations to readers. It is sold with the understanding that the writers, authors or publisher is not engaged to render any type of psychological, legal, or any other kind of professional advice. No warranties or guarantees are expressed or implied by the choice to include any of the content in this book. Neither the publisher nor the author or writers shall be liable for any physical, psychological, emotional, financial, or commercial damages including but not limited to special, incidental, consequential or other damages.

PRINTED IN THE UNITED STATES OF AMERICA

CONTENTS

INTRODUCTION

1	Overview	1
2	The role of stress	5
3	The role of resilience	7
4	The role of strategies	9

STRATEGIES

1	Create a care plan	13
2	Trauma input	17
3	Trauma filter	19
4	Debriefing	21
5	Mindful decon	25
6	Vagus nerve stimulation	27
7	Havening	29
8	Tapping	31
9	Imagery	33
10	Cognitive reappraisal	35
11	Sensory therapy	37
12	Chromotherapy	39
13	Laugh therapy	45
14	Hug therapy	49
15	Forest therapy	51
16	Dance/movement therapy	53
17	Crown massage	57
18	Music therapy	59
19	Doodle therapy	61
20	Belly breathing	63
21	Creating possibilities protocol	65
22	Progressive muscle relaxation	67
23	Baking therapy	69
24	How to sleep well	71
25	Bonus tips	73
	Resources	77
	About	85

CHAPTER 1
Overview

A disorder that affects those who do their work well.
DR. CHARLES FIGLEY

Long days. Irregular hours. Serving traumatized families with few breaks. These are key ingredients in the funeral industry that fuel the perfect storm called compassion fatigue. Also known as vicarious trauma, it is secondary traumatic stress absorbed by repeat exposure to grieving families without taking time to refuel the heart and decontaminate the mind. In short, compassion fatigue is a disorder that develops from doing your best funeral work without charging your own batteries.

A noble profession, the funeral industry expects a great deal from its members, including a strong sense of decorum, compassion, empathy, and common sense. Such a busy profession leaves little time for self-care. Yet, when funeral professionals are unable to recharge their internal battery between families or at the end of the day, the emotional residue of secondary traumatic stress can erode one's mental, emotional, and physical health, making it critical for funeral professionals to take steps to guard against it.

KEYNOTE

- Vicarious trauma is the cumulative effect of working with survivors.
- It is characterized by deep emotional and physical exhaustion.
- Symptoms resemble depression and PTSD.
- It can strike the most caring professionals.

THE COST OF CARING

Anyone who cares for others as part of their professional responsibilities is someone who has a higher risk of suffering from compassion fatigue. By the numbers (Gaille, 2017):

- 87% of emergency responders have reported symptoms of compassion fatigue.
- 70% of mental health professionals have experienced compassion fatigue.
- 1 in 2 child welfare workers experience symptoms of compassion fatigue in the severe range.
- Compassion fatigue has not been studied among funeral directors.

HOW IT HAPPENS

Compassion fatigue develops from unmitigated stress. To fully understand how it develops and how to mitigate against it, we examine three key pillars: (1) the role of stress, (2) the role of hormones, and (3) the role of resilience.

Symptoms

> **MOTHER TERESA**
>
> Mother Teresa mandated her nuns to take an entire year off from their duties every 4-5 years to allow them to heal from the effects of their care-giving work (Stress.org).

Symptoms of compassion fatigue can be subtle or stark. Below are the most common signs to look for.

- Emotional exhaustion & irritability
- Physical exhaustion
- Mental exhaustion
- Difficulty concentrating & clinical errors
- Lapse in judgment with client boundaries
- Reduced sense of meaning in work
- Struggle to complete assignments and tasks
- Lack of flexibility
- Dreading work

Compassion fatigue vs burnout

Compassion fatigue and burnout share many of the same symptoms. So, what's the difference?

- ✓ Compassion fatigue has a more rapid onset.
- ✓ Burnout is a slow burn that emerges over time.
- ✓ When managed early, compassion fatigue has a faster recovery.

The cost

How compassion fatigue affects funeral homes:

- ✓ Absenteeism
- ✓ Presenteeism
- ✓ Decreased productivity
- ✓ Clinical errors
- ✓ Lapse in judgment
- ✓ High turnover rate
- ✓ Cost to Corporate America: $48 billion per year (Gaille, 2017)

Management

Because compassion fatigue occurs when we help others without recharging our own batteries, proactively managing stress before it gets out of control builds positive buffering habits that can ultimately help to avoid prolonged stress and compassion fatigue.

Your funeral home has an invested interest in you taking care of both yourself and their families. You can't pour from an empty cup, nor would they want you to. If you feel the symptoms of compassion fatigue or emotional burnout, it's important to share this with your management. The longer you let it go, the harder it can be to recover from. On the following pages are strategies and management tips to help mitigate compassion fatigue symptoms before they lead to burnout.

EASY MANAGEMENT HOW-TO

- ✓ Understand how stress affects you
- ✓ Understand how resilience can offset stress and compassion fatigue
- ✓ Engage in activities that trigger the brain to secrete positive hormones
- ✓ Set emotional boundaries
- ✓ Maintain a healthy work-life balance
- ✓ Stay hydrated
- ✓ Eat for health
- ✓ Strive for restorative sleep

FOR SUPERVISORS

The wealth of every company is built on the health of its employees. Investing in your staff's emotional well-being is an investment in your business, and any good strategic plan starts from the top down. How can you help them adopt self-care strategies?

- ✓ Walk around to check in on staff. How are they doing?
- ✓ Suggest mini breaks throughout the day for forest therapy, laugh yoga, a healthy snack.
- ✓ Engage in team huddles to informally debrief and support each other.
- ✓ Create a staff support group.
- ✓ Designate one room as a Zen Zone or Quiet Room, and stock it with aromatherapy, music options, stress toys, etc.
- ✓ Give staff the tools and resources they need to do their jobs. Celebrate individual and collective successes.

NOTES:

CHAPTER 2

The role of stress

It's not stress that kills us. It's our reaction to it.
HANS SELYE

Types of stress

Stress is the body's neurobiological reaction to any change that requires an adjustment. It's the body's natural response to positive experiences as well as our natural defense against real or imagined danger. Though the nature and scope of stress differs, the brain uses hormones to respond.

EUSTRESS

Positive stress that keeps us alert, safe and motivated.

- Marriage
- Promotion
- New baby
- Winning money
- Moving
- Graduation

DISTRESS

Negative stress that wears down our physical and mental reserves.

- Divorce
- Punishment
- Injury
- Ill loved one
- Financial strain
- Long unpredictable

SECONDARY TRAUMATIC STRESS

Emotional residue from repeated secondary exposure to trauma. Professionals at risk include:

- Grief specialists
- Funeral professionals
- Human service workers
- Healthcare workers
- First responders
- Therapists & clinicians

Role of Hormones

The body uses hormones to help us respond, manage, and adjust to different situations, including those involving eustress, distress, and secondary traumatic stress.

Stress triggers our sympathetic nervous system to release stress hormones which then ignite a range of physiological changes, such as increased blood pressure, increased pulse, and more. When this happens, nonessential activities like digestion are put on standby.

POSITIVE HORMONES:
- Oxytocin (love)
- Dopamine (pleasure)
- Serotonin (happy)

STRESS HORMONES:
- Adrenaline (energy surge)
- Cortisol (stress)
- Norepinephrine (arousal)

Our fight-flight-freeze response is fired up by stressors, which triggers the brain to release 120 different chemicals, including stress hormones cortisol and adrenaline.

While these short-term changes help us cope, chronic activation of stress hormones like adrenaline and cortisol stop helping us and start being destructive to our bodies. Being in a constant state of stress increases the strain on our hearts, suppresses our immune system, and increases inflammation (Juster, McEwen, & Lupien, 2010; Schneiderman et al., 2005).

Meet Amy(gdala)

The amygdala, otherwise known as Amy, is a set of almond-shaped regions on each side of the brain. Serving as an internal alarm, Amy is triggered by stress, anxiety, fear and anger. When Amy senses stress, trauma, or a perceived threat, she signals our brain to release stress hormones that enable our body to either fight or freeze for survival, or flee to safety. Those same hormones anesthetize the brain's frontal lobes, disabling critical thinking and problem-solving skills.

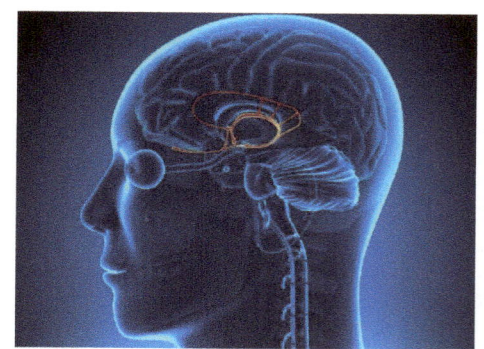

In essence, Amy and her band of stress hormones have hijacked the brain.

Chronic activation of Amy can lead to stress-induced plasticity in the brain with long-term consequences. The good news is that learning how to reactivate the frontal lobes through proactive strategies can be done through a conscious effort to calm down and restore logical thinking by engaging in modalities that deactivate Amy and/or trigger endorphins. Learning to reduce stress through adopted resilience strategies can create new healthy pathways in the brain that help us feel better. When we feel better, we cope better.

CHAPTER 3

The role of resilience

**Life doesn't get any easier or more forgiving.
We get stronger and more resilient.**

JAMAIS CASCIO

Human resilience is the ability to withstand, adapt to, or rebound from adversity through self awareness and pro-active strategies. How does this apply to the funeral profession? Funeral professionals tend to compartmentalize, and the strong sense of decorum requires the display of little emotion when doing their job. Yet, repeat triggering of the amygdala in response to exposure to trauma, long irregular hours, unpredictable breaks, and the constant output of empathy during a pandemic coupled with a surge in mass casualty incidents is changing the way funeral professionals think about self-care.

KEYNOTE

Proactively developing and regularly practicing positive stress-buffering habits can offset the stress hormones.

Role of resilience

Resilience is the ability to resist, recover from, or adapt to difficulties. When faced with a challenge, there are three possible outcomes:

1. Full recovery and ability to function
2. Partial recovery and stunted ability to function
3. No recovery and halted function (burnout)

Stress management and human resilience are complementary. Building and strengthening resilience through strategies that support the brain, body, and emotions can help mitigate stress, and prevent compassion fatigue and burnout.

HOW TO STRENGTHEN RESILIENCE

Step 1:
Learn to understand stress and how it affects you.

Step 2:
Take good care of yourself. We can't always predict stress and the outcome, but we are in control of how we care for ourselves mentally, physically, emotionally, and spiritually. Nurturing these areas can strengthen our ability to cope.

Step 3:
Use evidence-based modalities to deactivate the amygdala.

Step 4:
Use evidence-based modalities to trigger the brain to release positive hormones to offset stress hormones.

GOAL:
To build resilience, foster emotional recovery and a return to full function before the secondary traumatic stress affects your well-being.

KEYNOTE

Understanding how stress and vicarious trauma affects you personally, and learning to manage it proactively, will help build resilience against compassion fatigue and career burnout.

CHAPTER 4

The role of strategies

Nothing can wear you out like caring about people.
S.E. HINTON

The funeral industry is built on human compassion and desire to serve families in their darkest hour. Although most people experience normal stress, the funeral industry is a noble profession that requires long hours and unpredictable cases. Missed family events, sleep deprivation, and daily trauma cases provide the perfect petri dish for stress to grow, taking a toll on one's mental, physical and spiritual health. The good news is that stress can be mitigated by tapping into modalities you enjoy.

There are numerous strategies designed to take care of yourself, reduce stress, and mitigate compassion fatigue and burnout. Explore the 25 strategies contained in this manual and add those to your toolbox that you're most likely to engage with in the long run.

The key to each strategy is intentional practice. Like a muscle, the more you exercise it the stronger it becomes. Many strategies can become second nature, making it easy for you to stay on top of stress before it escalates.

Choose a proactive stance on mental conditioning over a reactive stance to crisis.

NOTES:

The ABCDs of prevention

Before building your toolbox of self-care techniques, evaluate your personal ABCDs of self care by answering the questions below.

A = AWARENESS

- What type of cases do you take home with you?

- What type of cases contribute to your stress level and increase your vulnerability to compassion fatigue?

- What external stressors are going on in your life?

B = BALANCE

- How do you set emotional boundaries? How often do you set these boundaries?

- How do you minimize external stress?

- What restores and replenishes you?

C = CONNECTIONS

- How strong is your support system?

- What connections do you have to like-minded activity groups?

D = DECONTAMINATION

- What mindful strategies or rituals do you use to decontaminate your mind and separate work from home?

_____

_____

Once you've answered the questions above, move on to strategy #1 to inventory the current tools in your toolbox that satisfy your emotional, physical, social and spiritual needs. Then consider augmenting with the evidence-based modalities in this manual to help build resilience and reduce stressors in your life that impact your work. Pair the modalities you're most likely to engage in with other fun activities to keep it fresh.

STRATEGY #1

Create a care plan

The love in the world begins with the love within ourselves.
DEEPAK CHOPRA

Self-care can improve your well-being, minimize stress, and reduce the opportunity for emotional burnout. Create a plan that triggers the brain's positive hormones and tends to your needs. This will help offset stress hormones, strengthen your ability to juggle demands, anchor your resilience, and prevent compassion fatigue from taking hold.

AIMS OF SELF CARE

- ✓ To help manage stress.
- ✓ To prevent physical illness.
- ✓ To protect inner resilience.
- ✓ To help maintain equilibrium.
- ✓ To maintain effectiveness and success.
- ✓ To ensure you live a meaningful life and honor one's own needs.

HOW TO BEGIN

Begin your care plan by identifying your physical, social, emotional and spiritual needs using the prompts below. Then list your personal strategies for how to fulfill those needs on page 15. Add things you enjoy to create a plan you're more likely to stick with.

PHYSICAL NEEDS

Nourishing your body with oxygen, hydration, and healthful food will help you physically feel better. When you feel better, you cope better.

- ❑ Practice good sleep hygiene, stay hydrated and eat for health.
- ❑ Move large muscles of the body through light exercise, housekeeping or dancing.
- ❑ Enjoy a good belly laugh at least once daily.
- ❑ Engage in physical outlets such as walking, hiking, yoga, swimming, etc.

SOCIAL NEEDS

Our social needs are met through fulfilling engagements and nurturing interactions.

- ❏ Attend community activities.
- ❏ Develop friendships that are supportive.
- ❏ Take or teach a self enrichment class.
- ❏ Join a book, tennis, quilt or knitting club.
- ❏ Travel.

EMOTIONAL NEEDS

Our emotional needs are met through empathy, understanding, and support from others.

- ❏ Create a trauma filter.
- ❏ Engage in debriefing after a traumatic case.
- ❏ Surround yourself with nurturing coworkers.
- ❏ Talk to loved ones about your feelings.
- ❏ Express your emotions in a journal.
- ❏ Engage in calming outlets such as coloring, knitting, gardening, puzzles, etc.

SPIRITUAL NEEDS

Our spiritual needs are met through inner reflection.

- ❏ Each day write down one thing you're grateful for.
- ❏ Try spiritual journaling.
- ❏ Try laughter yoga or forest therapy.
- ❏ Talk to clergy or a spiritual mentor.
- ❏ Engage in reflective practices such as prayer or meditation.

TIPS TO CREATING A GOOD SELF-CARE ROUTINE

- ✓ Make yourself your own best friend.
- ✓ Find someone to talk to.
- ✓ Stay nourished & hydrated.
- ✓ Practice good sleep hygiene.
- ✓ Minimize other forms of stress.
- ✓ Keep a light calendar.
- ✓ Engage in light exercise.
- ✓ Pursue a relaxing hobby such as knitting, clay work, drawing, beading, woodworking.
- ✓ Use evidence-based strategies to reduce stress.

MY CARE PLAN

STEP 1:
Consider and identify your emotional, physical, social and spiritual needs on the prior two pages. Add your own if they aren't listed.

STEP 2:
Draft your strategies below for how to engage in those activities. Using endorphin-boosting modalities you enjoy will trigger your brain's positive hormones to help offset stress hormones. Pair evidence-based modalities with other fun activities to keep it fresh.

STEP 3:
Put it into action and stick to it. Repetition is key to creating new pathways in the brain.

STEP 4:
Reassess every 3 months and adjust as needed.

MY PHYSICAL STRATEGIES:
1. _____
2. _____
3. _____
4. _____

MY EMOTIONAL STRATEGIES:
1. _____
2. _____
3. _____
4. _____

MY SOCIAL STRATEGIES:
1. _____
2. _____
3. _____
4. _____

MY SPIRITUAL STRATEGIES:
1. _____
2. _____
3. _____
4. _____

NOTES:

STRATEGY #2

Trauma Input

Every day in our caregiving role we empty out in order to be present to those in our care.

PATRICIA SMITH

Our brain is hardwired to be empathetic, yet we can maintain control over our empathy by filtering incoming data. It's important to recognize the amount of trauma information we unconsciously absorb throughout the day. Take an honest look at the amount of traumatic news you are exposed to through television, radio, social media, and conversations and take steps to minimize that exposure by changing the channel.

KEYNOTE

What are your barriers to taking proactive steps to mitigate stress?

Consider what you can and can't do to help yourself.

ASSESS YOURSELF

- ❏ Does your day begin with the morning news? How many difficult stories and disturbing images do you come across?
- ❏ At work, how many difficult stories do you hear outside your own client work?
- ❏ After work, do you listen to the news on the way home or watch it on TV at night?
- ❏ If you have a spouse who is also in the helping field, do you talk shop?

FROM DISTRESS TO EUSTRESS

Assessing our trauma input is only part of the equation. The second part—and perhaps the most important—is taking proactive steps to mitigate it. Consider it part of your overall wellness plan, and give it the same priority as your physical health.

NOTES:

STRATEGY #3

Create a trauma filter

Trauma fractures comprehension as a pebble shatters a windshield. The wound at the site of impact spreads across the field of vision, obscuring reality.

JANE LEAVY

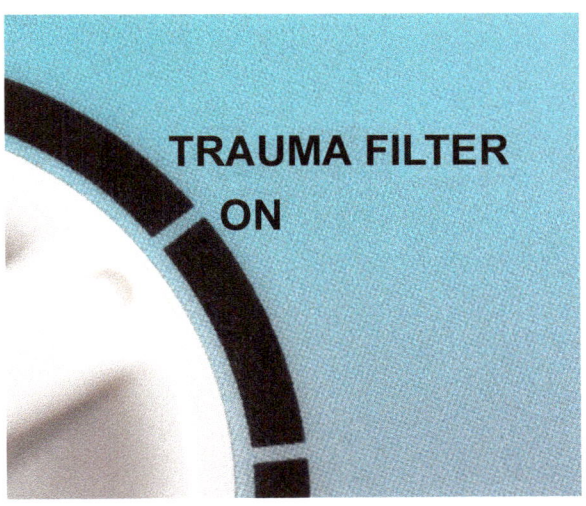

Because our brain is hardwired to be empathetic, when listening, we often create mental images to help us follow the storyline. Visualizing traumatic pictures can throw us off stride and contaminate the mind. Fortunately, to understand a client's situation, it isn't necessary to picture it. A trauma filter helps our brain maintain control over empathy by filtering incoming data from the story.

> **TIP**
>
> When working with a family, maintain awareness of your body's sensations and expressions. Check yourself:
>
> ♦ Are you taking shallow breaths?
>
> ♦ Is your pulse rapid?
>
> ♦ Are you leaning into your client's bubble?

- ✓ **Listen to client's story without visualizing it.** Imagine the trauma happening on a movie screen to distance yourself from the emotional impact.

- ✓ **Maintain a calm sense of detachment.** By sitting close to your client, mirroring his or her gestures and facial expressions, you come to feel nearly what your client is feeling. To be of any help, one person, however sympathetic to the plight of the other, needs to maintain a sense of calm detachment.

- ✓ **Put a physical barrier between you and your client** such as a stack of books, a desk, or a short floral bouquet on the coffee table between you.

- ✓ **Do you have your own shadow ACE** (adverse childhood experience) or that of someone you love that might have a hidden emotional impact? If so, resolve to seek therapy to reconciliate it. This will prevent it from looming again in your work.

- ✓ Give yourself *quiet time* each day. Turn off the news, and take a break from your phone. Studies have proven that phone addiction increases stress. Screen time may also negatively affect sleep. Making changes to daily habits that minimize constant stimuli can help us feel better.

NOTES:

STRATEGY #4

Debriefing

Well-being debriefings offer a powerful remedy that should be standard practice.
VICKIE LEFF, LCSW

Debriefing is a confidential discussion for staff dealing with an emotionally charged case, such as preparing a funeral for an abused child or the victim of a sensationalized crime.

How it works

Originating in the military years earlier, the first psychological debriefing model was officially developed in 1974 by Dr. Jeffrey Mitchell to provide quick intervention for those responding to psychological trauma by giving them the opportunity to release some of the emotional steam.

KEYNOTE

If your organization isn't comfortable facilitating an in-house debriefing, call International Grief Institute for assistance.

Now used around the world, debriefings provide a safe and secure environment for staff to process emotions associated with the event, and provide a supportive atmosphere. Because the wealth of a company is built on the health of its employees, debriefings can be crucial in that they invite staff to release emotional steam, minimizing opportunity for unhealthy coping strategies.

DEBRIEFING GOALS

- Mitigate emotional stress
- Reduce the impact of an upsetting case
- Facilitate normalization of work
- Serve as a forum for stress education
- Identify external coping resources

Although debriefings have historically been used with first responders, a modified debriefing is incredibly useful to address upsetting cases in the funeral home. Studies show that staff who undergo debriefing in the workplace within a 72-hour period experience less short- and long-term psychological trauma (Mitchell, 1988; Young, 1994).

Following are scripts and steps to facilitate a debriefing for your staff.

Debriefing Control keys

- ✓ Offer circle seating when possible to increase communication and decrease authority.
- ✓ Participation is mandatory.
- ✓ Rank is not recognized.
- ✓ Allow a couple of hours just to be safe. You don't want staff to feel rushed through the process.
- ✓ Listen and observe without judgment.
- ✓ Conflict must be minimized.
- ✓ Do not critique.

AGENDA

- ❏ Welcome everyone.
- ❏ Establish ground rules (see below).
- ❏ Share facts.
- ❏ Open the floor and allow for sharing.
- ❏ Keep on task.
- ❏ Sum up thoughts.
- ❏ Thank staff for being there.
- ❏ Respect confidentiality of debriefing process.

GROUND RULES

- ✓ Please silence all cellphones.
- ✓ Confidentiality is 100%. Anything shared here stays here.
- ✓ Everyone will have a chance to speak.
- ✓ Nobody is required to speak.
- ✓ Do not monopolize the conversation.
- ✓ Do not interrupt others.
- ✓ Respect. Do not judge another's feelings, story, or experience. Everyone has a right to express what they feel.
- ✓ Honor different beliefs and circumstances.
- ✓ Do not give advice. Share only your experience and emotions.
- ✓ Support one another as a team.
- ✓ Stay neutral. Feelings and emotions are not to be judged good nor bad.

Facilitating the process

STEP #1:
- Make everyone comfortable.
- Communicate ground rules.
- Thank everyone for attending.
- Validate individual emotions.

STEP #2
- Encourage participation.
- Agree to disagree.
- Honor staff members' time.
- View it as a team-building exercise.

STEP #3
- Listen.
- Scan the room.
- Look at body language.
- Check understanding; make no assumptions.
- Restate what you hear.

STEP #4
- Guide.
- Keep time.
- No "hogging" of the floor.
- Refer to the guidelines.
- Keep group in a safe, no judgment zone.

SCRIPT EXAMPLE:

This is a staff debriefing to help you process an upsetting case. We recognize this is a tough one. Your participation here will help fellow staff feel not so alone with their own emotions. People often differ in their responses to tough cases. You do not have to be experiencing any particular difficulty to benefit from this meeting. There are no specific expectations for you aside from the ground rules.

Before we begin, please allow me to share the ground rules.

- There is no rank during this discussion. Everyone is seen as equals.
- Please silence all phones, radios, electronic devices.
- Sharing is encouraged but voluntary. You do not need to share if you do not want to.
- One person at a time speaks.
- This is not a critique so please refrain from judgmental comments, even if recollections and thoughts differ from your experience. [A critique of the case, if needed, is done another time]
- This is confidential. No notes are kept and what is said here stays here.

The main part of this meeting is a discussion of the impact this case has had on you. Our objective is to help you ventilate some of the intense reactions and thoughts, and offer support.

We'll begin by going around the circle. [Ask each question below one at a time, then proceed around the table for answers before moving to the next question.]

1. **"Please briefly describe the case from your perspective."** [It is easier for people to discuss the facts first before moving on to the emotional aspect. Details are not necessary. There is no "reliving" the event.]

2. **"What was your first or most prominent thought when the case came in?"** [The above question transitions the staff from the cognitive (intellectual) domain to the affective (emotional) domain.]

3. **"What was the worst or hardest part of this case for you?"** [This question invites a frank answer, and may contain the most emotional content.]

4. **"What kind of symptoms have you encountered since? What emotions are hardest to deal with?"** [This provides an opportunity to externalize how the case is affecting each staff member.]

[Bring staff back to the cognitive domain by answering questions not already discussed. Be ready to distribute stress-reducing modalities (such as the ones included in this manual) and then bring to a close.]

Thank you for participating. We know this is a hard one. If you find yourself continuing to struggle, let us know and we'll arrange for a referral if necessary or requested. [End of meeting]

STRATEGY #5

Mindful decon

To increase our objectivity, we must learn to switch off the mini-movies. Objectivity requires us to be mindful, present in the moment, and experiencing what is happening without judgment.
ELIZABETH THORNTON

Firefighters decontaminate after a haz-mat situation. Nurses decontaminate wounds. Schools decontaminate surfaces. Mindful decon is a proactive strategy that decontaminates the mind after stress and trauma.

By nature, funeral professionals tend to do severe compartmentalization, show little emotion when doing the job for fear of looking unprofessional. Yet when left unmitigated, the continual compartmentalization of high stress can lead to chronic fatigue. By developing awareness, we can learn to regulate our stress reactions, and build resilience to support our behavioral, cognitive, emotional, physical and spiritual well-being.

> **KEYNOTE**
>
> What's the difference between mindful decon and self care?
>
> Mindful decon is self decontamination of the mind, an important element of self-care.

How it works

Continually working with traumatized families requires more processing than simple self-care. Funeral professionals are in active battle against stress, which requires special tools to self regulate while maintaining a battle-ready mindset.

Mindful decon is a proactive approach that uses techniques to decontaminate the mind after stress and trauma, and maintain mental fitness. By developing awareness, we can learn to regulate our stress reactions and build resilience to support our wellbeing. Practiced regularly, these techniques can decrease cumulative stress while laying a healthy foundation to process stress moving forward.

EASY MINDFUL DECON HOW-TO

Find your favorite way to decontaminate, and make it a pre- and post-shift practice.

- Trauma filter (page 19).
- Debriefing (page 21).
- Doodling. Doodling engages the creative side of our brain, and the repetitive hand motion induces a meditative theta brain wave (page 61).
- Crown massage (page 57).

> **KEYNOTE**
>
> "One of the critical ways to mitigate compassion fatigue is to take care of yourself."
>
> AMERICAN PSYCHOLOGICAL ASSOCIATION

> STRATEGY #6

Vagus nerve stimulation

In every heart there is a secret nerve that answers to the vibrations of beauty.
CHRISTOPHER MORLEY

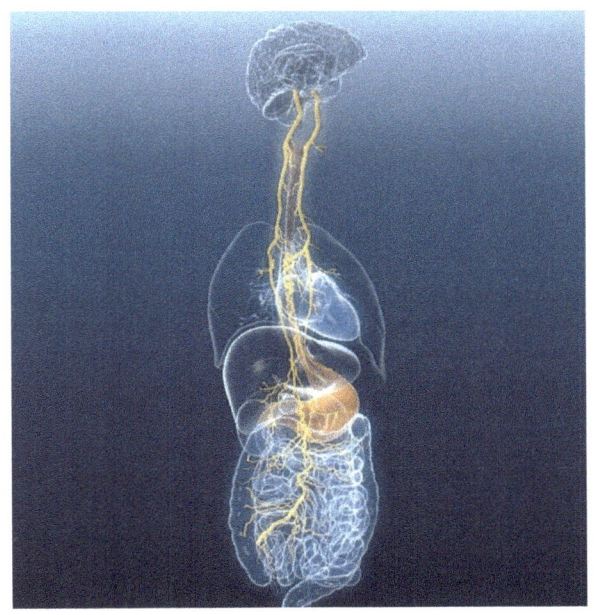

The longest nerve of the autonomic nervous system, the vagus nerve carries sensory information to the brain. It originates in the brain stem and extends down through the neck and chest into the abdomen.

How it works

Stimulating the vagus nerve produces what is called a vasovagal reflex, which lowers the blood pressure and slows the heart rate, deactivates Amy, and helps us to calm down.

EASY VAGUS NERVE STIMULATIONS

When we're stressed and jacked up, our breathing gets shallow. As a baby, we came into this world breathing from the belly, and belly breathing hits the vagus nerve. When you intentionally stimulate the vagus nerve, you can slow your heart rate and calm down. Easy ways to stimulate the vagus nerve include:

- Humming and singing.
- Yawning.
- "Arrrrrrrr," sounding like a pirate hits the back of the throat.

VALSALVA MANEUVER

The Valsalva maneuver is a vagus nerve technique that can slow your heart when it's beating too fast by creating a forceful strain that triggers your heart to calm down.

1. Take a deep breath and hold it.
2. Bear down hard, as if you're having a bowel movement.
3. While you're bearing down, breathe out like you're trying to blow up a balloon.
4. Strain hard for about 10 seconds.

> **IMPORTANT**
>
> Do not stimulate the vagus nerve if you struggle with low blood pressure.
> **Doing so can cause you to faint.**

NOTES:

STRATEGY #7

Havening

One touch of nature makes the whole world kin.
WILLIAM SHAKESPEARE

Havening is a psychosensory action involving touch to create delta brainwaves for therapeutic purposes. It helps build resilience, and is especially helpful for those in high-stress funeral careers.

How it works

Havening touch sends signals via skin receptors and nerves that are specialized to recognize a soothing touch and are hardwired in the brain. The brain receives the message produced by the hormone serotonin to calm down and relax.

Havening is like CPR for the amygdala, the fear center of the brain, by giving the brain a different job. Relying on the brain's neuroplasticity to rewire through consistent practice, havening can be done anytime and anywhere with no special skills.

EASY HAVENING HOW-TO

1. Gently rub your hands slowly for 2 to 3 minutes, as if washing them. Apply a nicely scented moisturizer or hand cream to heighten the skin receptors.
2. Imagine giving yourself a hug. Cross your arms over your chest so your hands rest on the opposite shoulder. Start at the shoulders and stroke your hands downward.
3. Stroke your face starting from the hairline and running your hands down your cheeks, as if rubbing in lotion.
4. Adding affirmations helps. Try repeating, "I am peaceful. I am calm," as you do the havening movements.

NOTES:

STRATEGY #8

Tapping

We all have that superhero inside us, but it's about tapping into it and embracing it and owning it.

NAFESSA WILLIAMS

The effects of stress can be diminished with a simple self-regulation psychosensory technique called tapping. A form of psychological acupressure, tapping is a proven self-help method for relaxing emotional stress that you can perform anytime and anywhere.

EASY TAPPING HOW-TO

Gently think about what bothers you, and then in quick succession using two fingers firmly and rhythmically tap 15 times on the points below. Take two deep breaths, relax and repeat the sequence on the opposite side. Take two deep breaths and relax again when done.

1. Relax and take two deep breaths.
2. With one hand, tap the palm of the other in a karate chop. Repeat.
3. Use both hands to tap the inside of the eyes near the nasal bridge. Repeat.
4. Tap the outside of your eyes. Repeat.
5. Tap underneath your eyes. Repeat.
6. Tap underneath your nose, above your lip. Repeat.
7. Tap under your lip. Repeat.
8. Tap underneath your clavicles (collarbones). Repeat.
9. Cross your arms and tap underneath your armpits. Repeat.
10. Relax and take two deep breaths again.
11. Repeat tapping on the opposite side.

NOTES:

STRATEGY #9

Imagery

Logic will get you from A to B. Imagination will take you everywhere.

ALBERT EINSTEIN

The imagination is a powerful place. Often we allow ourselves to be horrified by worries but hesitate to allow our minds to go on a holiday. An emotion-oriented strategy, imagery activates the senses and induces a peaceful state of mind.

How it works

Various forms of imagery have been used for centuries, and the technique is an established approach in Chinese medicine and American Indian traditions as well as other healing and religious practices. In the 1970s, Dr. David Bressler and Dr. Martin Rossman began established guided imagery as an effective approach for the treatment of stress, chronic pain, cancer, and other serious illnesses. Their work led them to co-found the Academy for Guided Imagery in 1989. A mini-escape through imagery has shown to reduce stress (Varvogli & Darviri, 2011).

EASY IMAGERY HOW-TO

- Create a place in your mind that is gorgeously serene, feels and even smells and tastes wonderful.
- Allow yourself to be creative in developing your place without judgement, and fill it only with delightful experiences. Take time each day to imagine this place to give your brain a break from the stressors in your life.
- To get the most out of imagery, use all your senses.

NOTES:

STRATEGY #10

Cognitive reappraisal

Cognitive psychology has shown that the mind best understands facts when they are woven into a conceptual fabric.

STEVEN PINKER

One of the most effective emotion-regulation strategies is cognitive reappraisal (Webb et al., 2012). A powerful tool, cognitive reappraisal is an intentional attempt to reframe an event in order to reframe the emotions around it. Simply put, changing how you think about a situation will ultimately impact how you feel about it, and positive feelings leads to stronger coping skills.

NEGATIVE THOUGHTS	POSITIVE REFRAMING
"I'll never get this done on time. It just is not possible."	"I'll do the best I can to finish on time, and give myself grace if I don't."

EASY COGNITIVE APPRAISAL HOW-TO

1. **Appraise the situation.** When experiencing stress, it's essential to find the trigger. What is causing all your stress? Critical thinking can help find the balance between the actual and perceived problem.

2. **Eliminate the catastrophe.** Once you identify the trigger, develop alternative courses of action. It's easy to see things as black and white, but cognitive reappraisal relies on finding what's in the gray.

3. As you **examine the stress**, consider the following:
    - Is there anything I'm grateful for in this situation?
    - What do I stand to learn from this experience?
    - Do I have any prior knowledge that may help me move forward?

4. **Reassign emotions.** Use an optimistic inner dialogue to see the positives. Consciously reassigning the emotional impact with positive beliefs will improve your confidence to handle stress.

5. Finally, **acknowledge your achievements**. It's easy to focus on what you have left to do rather than what you've gotten done. Pat yourself on the back for achievements.

NOTES:

STRATEGY #11

Sensory therapy

A treat is a small pleasure that we give to ourselves.
GRETCHEN RUBIN

Our five senses play a role in how we feel, and can be influenced by what our senses take in. Sometimes when life feels stressful or hopeless, treat your five senses to something that looks, feels, smells, tastes, or sounds good. Treating ourselves to something that evokes sensorial joy stimulates our brain to release feel-good hormones that help offset stress hormones.

How it works

The sensation of pleasure triggers our brain to release happy hormones such as oxytocin, dopamine, and serotonin. Research also shows that in addition to the pleasure of taste, certain foods help reduce stress, including avocado, oatmeal, raspberries, blueberries, oranges, pistachios, walnuts, and chocolate.

> **ACTIVITY**
>
> **RULE OF 5s**
> Every day practice the Rule of 5 by enjoying the following:
> - 5 things you can **see**
> - 4 things you can **touch**
> - 3 things you can **hear**
> - 2 things you can **smell**
> - 1 thing you can **taste**

Find ways to offer yourself some form of sensorial pleasure every day. With practice, the awareness of delight eventually becomes effortless, and is an important step toward restoring balance in times of stress.

SIGHT—VISUAL SUGGESTIONS:

- Watch a sunrise or sunset
- Look at a cherished photo or a favorite memento
- Use a plant or flowers to enliven your work space
- Enjoy the beauty of a garden, the beach, a park, or your own backyard
- Surround yourself with colors that lift your spirits

TACTILE—TOUCH SUGGESTIONS:

- Soak in a warm tub with Epsom salts or bath oil
- Wear a pair of extra soft socks
- Wrap yourself in a soft scarf or blanket
- Pet a dog or cat

HEARING—SOUND SUGGESTIONS:

- Listen to relaxing or upbeat music
- Listen to laughter on YouTube or comedy show
- Listen to the sound of the ocean, waterfall, or fountain, or the birds singing
- Hang windchimes near a window

OLFACTION—SMELL SUGGESTIONS:

- Shower or bathe with a lovely scented soap
- Light a fragrant candle or burn incense
- Apply a scented lotion to your skin before bed
- Buy a fragrant flower bouquet for the kitchen or your office
- Experiment with different essential oils in a diffuser
- Enjoy clean, fresh air in the great outdoors
- Spritz on your favorite perfume

GUSTATION—TASTE SUGGESTIONS:

- Enjoy one of the foods listed on the prior page
- Enjoy a mug of herbal tea, cocoa with whipped cream, or a cold drink
- Chew flavored gum
- Indulge in a piece of dark chocolate
- Eat a ripe piece of fruit

STRATEGY #12

Chromotherapy

There is not one blade of grass, there is no color in this world that is not intended to make us rejoice.

JOHN CALVIN

Colors are all around us, and they aren't meaningless. They can change the way we feel and react. Although chromotherapy has been around since the time of Ancient Egypt, Western researchers are now adapting to the idea of chromotherapy as a healing modality, and studying the scientific properties of how colored lights affect our brain and emotions.

How it works

ACTIVITY

Grab your favorite adult coloring book or color the following pages using gel pens, crayons, colored pencils or felt tipped pens when you need to relax.

- Calms the amygdala
- Takes us outside the thinking part of our brain
- Certain colors can invigorate a depressed mind or soothe an agitated mind
- Lowers blood pressure
- Relaxes breathing
- The repetitive hand motions used in coloring a picture induces a meditative state

MORE METHODS OF USING COLOR TO FEEL LESS STRESSED

- Paint a color-by-number picture
- Color your bath water
- Plug in a colored nightlight
- Hang a colored glass prism
- Paint the walls of your bedroom or office
- Add colorful home décor
- Use colored bulbs in your lamps
- Enjoy a color wash YouTube video
- Download a color therapy app
- Enjoy a chromotherapy sauna

> **STRATEGY #13**

Laugh therapy

Laughter offsets the impact of mental stress.
MICHAEL MILLER, M.D.

Those who need a good laugh are usually the ones who feel least like laughing. A powerful healing modality, studies show that laughter offers many physical, psychological, emotional, and social benefits. It decreases stress and increases immune and infection-fighting antibodies.

How it works

Smiling and laughter stimulate the facial muscles that trigger the brain to release happy hormones called endorphins, the body's natural feel-good chemicals that promote an overall sense of well-being.

Because the body can't tell the difference between a real or fake smile, hold a pencil between your teeth to "fake it until you make it." The brain can't tell the difference and will be tricked into releasing those feel-good chemicals anyway.

No matter what you choose to induce a good belly laugh, the bottom line is that whatever makes you laugh is truly good medicine. How it works:

- 10 minutes of belly laughter is equivalent to 30 minutes on a cardiovascular machine.
- Laughter and crying are like yin and yang, they both release energy.
- Laughing bypasses the mind and helps us keep a positive attitude.
- Laughter creates the perfect diaphragmatic breath. When we laugh, we exhale completely and then inhale completely, which oxygenates the brain and body. When our brains are fully oxygenated, our minds become calm and clear.
- Laughter releases endorphins which help us feel good. The brain oxygenation and endorphins combination is like a joyful cocktail. When we feel good and the mind is clear, we feel grounded and peaceful, less stress and less reactive.

Psychological benefits

You can fake it until you make it. When you smile, the stimulation of the facial muscles in that way trigger the brain to release the hormones that cause the feeling of happiness. This works even if you weren't feeling happy in the first place. The phenomena is called Facial Feedback. This works especially well if you look at yourself in the mirror, as the visual cues reinforce to your brain that you're smiling and therefore must be happy.

Emotional health

Laughter makes us feel good, and this feeling can remain long after the laughter subsides. The American Psychological Association has stated that smiling as little as 20 minutes every day, even if faked, was effective in reducing symptoms of depression. Plus, because of the body's physiological reaction to smiling and laughing, it is impossible to fee anxious, angry or sad when we're laughing.

STRESS REDUCTION

Laughter helps release stress and increase energy. Clinical research has proven that laughter lowers the level of stress hormones in the blood.

POSITIVE COPING STRATEGY

Even in the most difficult of times, a laugh—or even simply a smile—can go a long way toward making us feel better. Laughter stimulates the brain into a positive state, which helps clear the mind and allow for clarity and focus. Laughter helps change our perspective. Laughing, especially when we're having a tough time, creates psychological distance and can slow the momentum of overwhelm, frustration or disappointment. By getting in a positive physical and emotional state, it triggers our mind to recall positive memories and have an optimistic outlook.

Laughter is contagious. Just hearing laughter primes our brain and readies us to smile and join in the fun. Laughing in a group can produce euphoric experiences as everyone else's laughter and joy becomes infectious, signaling our brain to let go and have a good time. Even just smiling or laughing by yourself, with others observing, can help boost their mood, too.

Studies have shown that happiness can double our critical thinking skills, problem solving, and creativity. It has been shown that the happier we are, the longer we live. And, it's been shown to create more fulfilling and longer lasting relationships, and more successful careers.

Physical benefits

CARDIO

Laughter is a great cardio workout, especially for those who are incapable of doing other physical activities due to injury or illness. It gets your heart pumping and burns a similar amount of calories per hour as walking at a slow to moderate pace. In fact, research have found that one minute of a good laugh is like a ten minutes on a rowing machine.

BLOOD PRESSURE

Laughter has demonstrated to be a great way to lower your blood pressure. Even if you have normal blood pressure, lowering it will reduce the risk of strokes and heart attacks. Researchers at the University of Maryland demonstrated the impact of laugher by showing two videos, a drama and a comedy. They determined that the comedies normalized blood vessels and increase blood flow, while drama restricted blood vessels.

IMMUNE RESPONSE

One of the best benefits of laughter is that it decreases your stress levels and increases your immune response. T-cells are specialized immune system cells just waiting for activation. When you laugh, you activate T-cells that immediately begin to help you fight off sickness Some studies have demonstrated that laughter increases levels of infection-fighting antibodies and boosts your levels of immune cells. So, if you feel a cold coming on, add laughter to your illness prevention plan.

BLOOD SUGAR

Studies into laughter have demonstrated that diabetics showed lower blood sugars levels after a laughter session than they did when eating the same thing and participating in a laughter session.

PAIN KILLER

Endorphins are the body's natural pain killers. By laughing, you release endorphins, which can help ease chronic pain and make you feel good all over.

CORE MUSCLES

One of the benefits of laughter is that it can help you tone your abs and strengthen core muscles. When you are laughing, the muscles in your stomach expand and contract, similar to when you intentionally exercise your abs. Meanwhile, the muscles you are not using to laugh are getting an opportunity to relax.

> **ACTIVITY**
>
> Enjoy a good belly laugh at least once daily.

How to laugh (when you don't feel like it):

- Watch a comedy movie or TV show
- Watch funny YouTube videos
- Listen to children laughing at the park
- Watch blooper reels on TV
- Read a funny book
- Look at funny pictures
- Read funny social media memes
- Listen to funny jokes

Laughter Yoga:

Laughter yoga was started by Dr. Madan Kataria, a physician from Mumbai, India, who launched the first laughter club at a park in 1995, with just 5 people. Within two weeks, he had 50 people. Now there are over 13,000 laughter clubs in 80 countries around the world.

HOW IT WORKS

- Helps to change your mood within minutes by releasing endorphins in your brain.
- It oxygenates the brain, making you feel more energetic and relaxed.
- It also strengthens your immune system.
- Laughter is a positive energy, and like attracts like.
- Allow yourself to let go, be silly, be playful.
- You can stay in your chair the whole time. No need to learn any hard yoga moves.
- Laughter helps to create a positive mental state to deal with negative situations and negative people.
- It gives hope and optimism to cope with difficult times.

STRATEGY #14

Hug therapy

We need 4 hugs a day for survival. We need 8 hugs a day for maintenance. We need 12 hugs a day for growth.

VIRGINIA SATIR

The average length of a hug between two people is 3 seconds. Research shows that a hug lasting at least 20 seconds has a therapeutic effect on the body and mind.

A sincere embrace produces the love hormone oxytocin which has many benefits in our physical and mental health. A natural tranquilizer, it helps us to relax, to feel safe and calm our fears and anxiety. And it's free every time we hug, cradle a child, cherish a dog or cat, slow dance, or simply hold the shoulders of a friend.

How it works

STIMULATES OXYTOCIN

Oxytocin is a neurotransmitter that acts on the limbic system, the brain's emotional center:
- promotes contentment
- reduces anxiety and stress
- it's known to make mammals monogamous
- Released during childbirth, helping mothers forget about the labor they endured and fall immediately in love with their newborn
- Lowers heart rate
- Lowers cortisol level (the hormone responsible for stress)

FOSTERS CONNECTIONS

Connections are fostered when people take the time to appreciate and acknowledge one another, and a hug is a free, easy, and—at 20 seconds—is a quick way to show love and appreciation.

Giving is good for the giver in that a hug benefits ourselves and others.

PREVENTS DISEASE

Affection also has a direct response on the reduction of stress which prevents many diseases. Touch Research Institute at the University of Miami School of Medicine has carried out more than 100 studies on the power of touch, and discovered evidence of improved immune system, reduced pain, lower glucose levels, and faster growth in premature babies.

STIMULATES THYMUS GLAND

Hugs apply gentle pressure on the sternum which stimulates the thymus gland, which regulates and balances the production of white blood cells, which keep you healthy and disease free.

NO WORDS NEEDED

Almost 70 percent of communication is nonverbal. Hugging is an excellent method of expressing yourself nonverbally to another human being or animal. Not only can they feel the love and care in your embrace, but they can actually be receptive enough to pay it forward to others.

BOOSTS SELF-ESTEEM

Hugging boosts self-esteem, especially in children. From the time we're born our family's touch shows us that we're loved and special. The associations of self-worth and tactile sensations from our early years become imbedded in our nervous system as we grow into adults. They become imprinted at a cellular level, and therefore connect us to our ability to self love.

STIMULATES DOPAMINE

Everything everyone does involves protecting and triggering dopamine flow. Low dopamine levels play a role in neurodegenerative diseases and mood disorders such as depression. Dopamine is responsible for giving us that feel-good feeling, and it's also responsible for motivation. Hugs stimulate the brain to release dopamine, the pleasure hormone.

STIMULATES SEROTONIN

Hugging releases endorphins and serotonin into the blood vessels which cause pleasure and negate pain and sadness. It also reduces the risk of heart problems, helps fight excess weight, and prolongs life. Hugging raises our serotonin levels, elevating mood and creating happiness.

PARASYMPATHETIC BALANCE

Hugs balance out the nervous system. Skin contains a network of tiny pressure centers that can sense touch and notify the brain through the vagus nerve. The galvanic skin response of someone receiving and giving a hug shows a change in skin conductance which suggests a more balanced state in the parasympathetic nervous system.

ACTIVITY

If you live alone, hug a stuffed animal, a pet, a blanket or pillow.

STRATEGY #15

Forest therapy

There are moments when all anxiety and stated toil are becalmed in the infinite leisure and repose of nature.
HENRY DAVID THOREAU

Forest therapy is rooted in the Japanese practice of Shinrin-yoku, which is often translated as "forest bathing."

Exposing your brain to restorative environments by immersing yourself in the atmosphere of the forest helps with mental fatigue by eliciting feelings of awe. One study found that people's mental energy bounced back even when they just looked at pictures of nature (Psychological Science, 2012).

Another study found that students sent into the forest for two nights had lower levels of cortisol, the stress hormone, than those who spent that time in the city. In another study, researchers found a decrease in both heart rate and levels of cortisol in subjects in the forest when compared to those in the city.

Even the view of nature out a window is associated with lower stress and higher job satisfaction (Scandinavian Journal of Forest Research, 2007; Environmental Health and Preventative Medicine, 2010; Japanese Journal of Hygiene, 2011; Biomedical and Environmental Sciences, 2012).

How it works

The natural environment is "restorative," and one thing that a walk outside can restore is your waning attention. In one study, researchers worked to deplete participants' ability to focus. Then some took a walk in nature, some took a walk through the city, and the rest just relaxed. When they returned, the nature group scored the best on a proofreading task.

Other studies have found similar results—even seeing a natural scene through a window can help.

Doses of nature have found to improve concentration after just 20 minutes in a park (Environment & Behavior, 1991; Journal of Environmental Psychology, 1995 (2); Journal of Attention Disorders, 2008).

HOW IT HELPS OUR MOOD

Stress, anxiety, and depression may all be eased by some time in the great outdoors, especially when combined with exercise.

One study found that walks in the forest were specifically associated with decreased levels of anxiety and bad moods, and another found that outdoor walks could be useful clinically. The effects of nearby water improves it even more.

EASY FOREST THERAPY HOW-TO

If you don't work or live near trees, try:

- ✓ Watch forest videos on YouTube
- ✓ Hang a forest picture on the wall
- ✓ Replace your computer's background image with a forest image

ACTIVITY

Take a 10-minute walk through trees every day.

STRATEGY #16

Dance/movement therapy

When you dance, your purpose is not to get to a certain place on the floor. It's to enjoy each step along the way.

DR. WAYNE DYER

Feelings can influence your movement, and movement can impact your feelings (and change your brain). When we feel tired and stressed, we tend to move more slowly. When we feel anxious, we may either rush around or become completely paralyzed.

If you tend to shut down when you're under stress, stress-relieving activities that get you moving yield many positive benefits.

ACTIVITY

Write down your favorite upbeat songs, and dance to one song every day.

How it works

Movement is one of the most basic functions of the human body, making it easy to find ways to incorporate motion into daily life in a way that feels good.

Dance/movement therapy (DMT) uses movement to help achieve emotional, cognitive, physical and social integration. Dancing benefits us both physically and mentally through stress reduction, mood management, increased mobility, decreased muscle tension, and more.

Dance/movement therapy can be used with all populations and with individuals, couples, families, or groups. In general, dance therapy promotes self-awareness, self-esteem, and a safe space for the expression of feelings.

MOTION AND EMOTIONS ARE INTERCONNECTED

The creative expression of dancing is commonly used to treat physical, psychological, cognitive, and social issues such as:

- Chronic pain
- Childhood obesity
- Cancer
- Arthritis
- Hypertension
- Cardiovascular disease
- Anxiety
- Depression
- Disordered eating
- Poor self-esteem
- Posttraumatic stress
- Dementia
- Communication issues
- Autism
- Aggression/violence
- Domestic violence trauma
- Social interaction
- Family conflict

ENHANCES YOUR MOOD

Moving your body improves your mood, and helps combat anxiety and stress. Data show that exercise provides these benefits both in healthy individuals as well as those with diagnosed emotional disorders, regardless of sex and age.

HEALTHIER LYMPH

The lymphatic system is an important part of your body's immune system. The lymph system is a series of channels and nodes dispersed throughout the body that move lymph fluid. Lymph fluid contains infection-fighting white blood cells throughout the body.

Unlike the circulatory or respiratory systems, the lymphatic system does not have a pump. It relies on our motion to circulate lymph fluid around the body. Each time we use large muscles, it helps pump lymphatic fluid through our body, keeping our systems circulating.

HEALTHIER BONES

After our thirties, bone mass starts to decline. When our muscles push and pull against bones, this helps to build and preserve bone mass. Any sustained activity such as walking, dancing, or taking the stairs, helps to build bone mass.

ENHANCED BRAIN HEALTH

Exercise improves cognitive performance for people of all ages. In one study, children who participated in physical activity demonstrated increased electrical activity in the brain, as well as improved mental accuracy and reaction times. Another study confirmed that a healthy workout routine early in life may help to predict our level of cognitive decline later in life.

IMPROVED SEX LIFE

Exercise through dancing improves arousal and satisfaction for both men and women. For men, not only does increased blood flow improve sexual function, but regular exercise also helps with psychosocial factors such as mood, stress, and confidence. For women, regularly moving the body may help to increase sexual function and arousal related to increased endorphins.

EASY HOW-TO

When dancing just isn't possible, consider the following alternatives:

- Run in place or jump up and down
- Stretch or roll your head in circles
- Go for a short walk
- Squeeze a rubbery stress ball
- Window shop
- Gardening
- Stretching
- Grocery shop with a basket instead of a cart
- Romp around with the kids or grandkids
- Walk, bike, or hike

NOTES:

STRATEGY #17

Crown massage

I take a massage each week. This isn't an indulgence, it's an investment in your full creative expression, productivity, passion and sustained good health.

ROBIN S. SHARMA

The prefrontal cortex is the center for logical thought. During stress, blood leaves this area to assist other areas for immediate action.

How it works

When we massage our scalp, we stimulate sensitive nerves that can calm our nervous system, reduce the level of stress hormones in our body, lower blood pressure, and even help us sleep. Research also suggests scalp massages can alleviate the pain and frequency of tension headaches.

The crown massage will bring the blood flow back to the prefrontal cortex, clearing the mind and calm the amygdala. The act of touch also satisfies skin hunger.

EASY HOW-TO

1. Place your thumbs on the temples with your fingers touching in the center of your forehead.

2. With a good amount of pressure, pull your fingers from the center of the forehead to the sides. Repeat for 30 to 60 seconds.

3. Finish by taking a comb or brush and run it from the front of your head to the nape of your neck.

NOTES:

STRATEGY #18

Music therapy

Music expresses that which cannot be said and on which it is impossible to be silent.
VICTOR HUGO

Most of us love a catchy song on the radio, and many of us have a favorite band or genre, and for good reason. Music affects our attention, emotion, behavior, cognition, and communication, and studies show it can bring about relaxation and pleasure (Koelsch et al., 2009).

How it works

Functional neuroimaging studies have shown that listening to music affects the limbic and paralimbic structures of the brain (Koelsch et al., 2009). In other words, music triggers activity in the same part of the brain that releases the pleasure hormone, dopamine. Further, music has the power to evoke and modulate emotions which affects the autonomic nervous system, endocrine system, and immune system.

BENEFITS

Major health benefits of music are (Levy, 2017):

- Music provides an outlet for expression of feelings
- Music reduces anxiety and physical effects of stress
- Our heartbeat can change to mimic the music we're listening to (Blodgett, 2015)
- It can help manage Parkinson's and Alzheimer's disease
- Music reduces depression
- It helps to reduce symptoms of psychological disorders including schizophrenia
- Music improves self-expression and communication

NOTES:

STRATEGY #19

Doodle therapy

We are visual creatures. When you doodle an image that captures the essence of an idea, you not only remember it, you also help other people understand and act on it.
TOM WUJEC

Stress can lead to a lack of concentration that can make it hard to focus on tasks. Doodling offers a distraction by taking our mind off hijacking stressors. Further, focusing on the movements of the pen coupled with repetitive hand motions can induce a meditative state.

How it works

Doodling, a form of art therapy, requires repetitive movements, which can build our attention span and improve our ability to concentrate. At their core, doodles are nonverbal messages that surface from the unconscious mind, and typically symbolize feelings and thoughts in visual form. While doodling, one need not worry about becoming an art connoisseur, rather it's an intentional act that simply takes our mind off of what bothers us.

BENEFITS

- Doodling offers your mind a creative outlet to express itself.

- One study showed that doodling while listening to someone on the phone, participants were able to recall 29% more material afterward compared to those who just took notes (Andrade, 2009).

- When doodling, your mind can tap into deeply held emotions and bring them to the surface. Over time, this promotes psychological homeostasis (Moore, 2017).

- For reasons not fully understood, doodling helps to generate fresh ideas. Because this activity distracts folks from focusing on a given problem, it allows the unconscious mind to kick it around and inspire solutions.

NOTES:

STRATEGY #20

Belly breathing

Every breath we take, every step we make, can be filled with peace, joy and serenity.

THICH NHAT HANH

As a baby, we came into this world breathing from the belly. As we grow and mature, we transition to chest breathing. Breathing from the chest only partially fills the lungs. Not getting enough oxygen keeps our body in a state of hyperarousal, making it difficult to relax.

How it works

Our bodies are designed to use our diaphragm for drawing in air. Using our diaphragm to breathe means drawing in air from the belly, allowing for full oxygenation of the lung lobes. Studies show that stress suppresses the immune system yet belly breathing can help lower stress (Harvard Health Publishing, 2020). Further, when you're focusing on your diaphragm, you're not focusing on stressors, and the full oxygenation clears your mind and tricks the brain into switching into parasympathetic mode. As the heart rate slows, the stress response will subside (American Lung Association, 2020).

4-4-8 BREATHING

This technique is like a vagal maneuver, though not as intense.

1. Using your belly to breathe, breathe in to the count of 4. Feel your abdomen expand.
2. Hold for a count of 4.
3. Release for the count of 8.
4. Repeat for 5 to 10 minutes.

NOTES:

STRATEGY #21

Creating possibilities protocol (CPP)

You can't change who you are, but you can change what you have in your head, you can refresh what you're thinking about, you can put some fresh air in your brain.

ERNESTO BERTARELLI

CPP is a neuroplasticity exercise that uses cognitive framing to enhance an emotion. This can be particularly helpful for those who struggle to believe affirmations about themselves or whose survival brain struggles to let go of the stress (Dr. Kate Truitt, 2020).

How it works

CPP empowers the amygdala and hippocampus to build positive and resilience-focused neuroplasticity tracks by identifying a desired emotion and then developing a connection to it using the following steps.

- Identify a desired emotion.
- Identify a time when you last felt that emotion. To strengthen the connection to this emotion, engage breathwork by inhaling to the count of 4, and exhaling to the count of 6.
- Create a what-if statement involving this emotion such as, "What if I was . . . " Repeat statement 5 times.
- Create an I-can statement, "I can be . . . " Repeat statement 5 times.
- Create an I-will statement, "I will be . . . ." Repeat statement 5 times.
- Create an I-am statement, "I am . . . " Repeat statement 5 times.

TIPS:

- Inhale through the nose to a count of 4. This slows breathing and welcomes calm.
- Exhale to a count of 6. Slower exhalation encourages deeper oxygenation of cells, and engages the parasympathetic nervous system.

NOTES:

STRATEGY #22

Progressive muscle relaxation

I think self-discipline is something, it's like a muscle. The more you exercise it, the stronger it gets.

DANIEL GOLDSTEIN

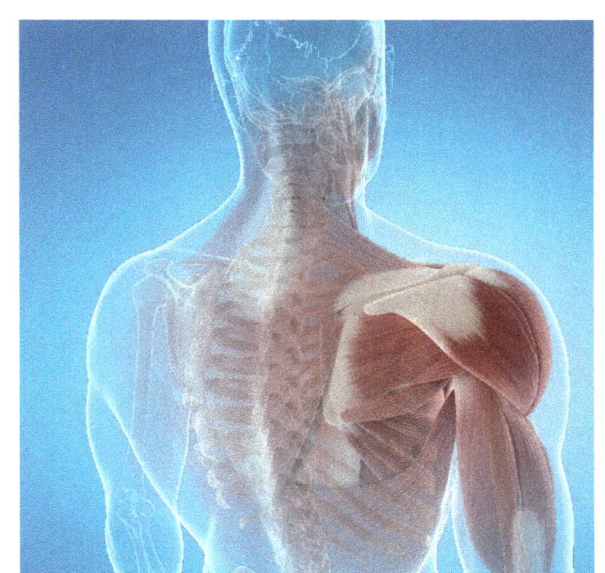

Progressive muscle relaxation (PMR) involves tightening then relaxing muscle groups, one after another. Upon steady practice, one can delineate between relaxed and tense muscles, and take action to calm muscles tensed from stress.

How it works

Progressive muscle relaxation exercises has been found to reduce cortisol levels, anxiety, heart rate, and blood pressure (Varvogli & Darviri, 2011). Upon steady practice, one can learn to recognize when muscles are tense from stress, and take action to calm them.

EASY PMR EXERCISE

- Before starting, find a comfortable position in a quiet place.
- Let your eyes close or find a point to look at without straining.
- Take several slow, deep breaths.
- Do the following for each of the muscle groups listed on the next page.
    1. Inhale and tighten one muscle or the group of muscles for approximately 5 seconds.
    2. Note how your body feels and what thoughts you have.
    3. Exhale and release the muscle for approximately 5 seconds.
    4. Notice how your body and mind feel.
    5. Move onto the next group of muscles and repeat steps 1-5.

MUSCLE GROUPS

Using the instructions on the prior page, move through the muscle groups listed below. Do left and right at the same time if able.

> **IMPORTANT**
>
> Check with your doctor before doing PMR if you have a muscle or bone injury, or recovering from surgery.

1. Hands: Clinch both hands into fists.
2. Arms (biceps): Bend your elbows 90 degrees and make a muscle.
3. Arms (triceps): Straighten your arms and tighten the backs of your arms.
4. Shoulders: Shrug both shoulders.
5. Forehead: Wrinkle your nose to wrinkle your forehead.
6. Eyes: Close your eyes tightly.
7. Jaw: Clench your jaw.
8. Mouth: Smile as big as you can.
9. Neck: Move your chin down to your chest then, on your next breath, look up above your head.
10. Lower back: Arch your back away from the ground or chair.
11. Abdomen/stomach: Tighten your stomach muscles.
12. Buttocks: Tighten your buttock muscles.
13. Thighs: Tighten your thighs; this may cause your legs to come off the ground.
14. Lower legs: Point your toes away from your head then, on your next breath, point them toward your head.

STRATEGY #23

Baking therapy

Cooking and baking is both physical and mental therapy.
MARY BERRY

Life isn't always a box of chocolate, though many of us wished it was. When feeling stressed, try baking.

How it works

Baking is a sensory experience that requires panning, concentration and mindfulness, which activates our brain. Kneading becomes meditation. The smell delights our olfactory. Clear instructions give a sense of order. And the end product rewards our tastebuds for a job well done.

If you want to slow down, try making a batch of caramels. If you like working with your hands, try making bread, cinnamon rolls, pizza crust, or try the easy shortbread recipe below.

SOOTHING SHORTBREAD

8 oz. butter
½ c. granulated sugar
1 ½ c. all-purpose flour
½ c. rice flour

DIRECTIONS

1. Cream butter and sugar. Add in both flours.
2. Roll dough into 1" balls and place on ungreased baking tray. Flatten slightly with a fork.
3. Bake at 325° for 10 minutes. Remove from oven and cool.

NOTES:

STRATEGY #24

Sleep well

When you have laboriously accomplished your daily task, go to sleep in peace.
VICTOR HUGO

Stress creates upheaval that can lead to many sleepless nights. Juggling such emotional strains often leads to serial tossing and turning, sleep disruption and insomnia. In turn, the ensuing sleep deprivation magnifies our emotions and reduces our ability to cope with stress, creating what feels like an unending circle.

WHY IT MATTERS

Studies show that receiving less than 7 hours of sleep at night may increase our risk of diabetes, heart conditions, obesity, or anxiety. Managing sleep disruption and insomnia by practicing good sleep hygiene, coupled with medical management when needed, can help restore a restful sleep pattern, and lead to significant improvements in other stress symptoms (National Institutes of Health, 2008).

ACTIVITY

Create a relaxing bedtime ritual to give your mind and body time to wind down. It sends a signal to your brain that bedtime is near, and trains it to go into quiet mode.

BENEFITS OF GOOD SLEEP HYGIENE

Healthy sleep habits are an essential part of caring for yourself, and can make a big difference in your quality of life. Studies show that good sleep helps you cope better in times of stress. It can also lower your blood pressure, improve your memory, help keep your immunity strong, and puts you in a better mood.

Known as good sleep hygiene, healthy bedtime habits can influence the body's circadian rhythms. Healthy daytime habits, including what you eat, drink, how much daylight and physical exercise you get, also play roles.

SLEEP HYGIENE TIPS

Try the following suggestions from the National Sleep Foundation to help you reestablish a restorative sleep pattern.

- To help regulate your body's clock, stick to a sleep schedule of the same bedtime and wake time, even on weekends.
- Exercise early in the day. Vigorous exercise is best, but even light exercise is better than no exercise.
- A sleep environment between 60 and 67 degrees is ideal.
- If your partner snores, consider using a fan, earplugs, or white noise.
- Use comfortable pillows and bed linen.
- Consider moving around the bedroom furniture, repainting the bedroom walls, and purchasing new bed linen.
- Avoid bright light in the evening to keep your circadian rhythm in check.
- Avoid alcohol, caffeine, cigarettes, and heavy meals later in the day.
- Try wearing a sleep mask or weighted blanket across your feet to help reduce stimuli and calm your mind.

If you continue to struggle with sleepless nights after trying the tips above, cognitive behavioral therapy is one of the top suggestions for treating long-term sleep disruption. Speak to your doctor to learn more about this process.

STRATEGY #25

BONUS TIPS

Every day is a bonus.
GEOFFREY BOYCOTT

MORE WORKPLACE STRATEGIES TO REDUCE STRESS

- Chew gum. A stick of gum can lower cortisol levels.

- Stomp on bubble sheets.

- Eat chocolate. Just one square can calm your nerves by regulating levels of cortisol.

- Eat honey. Honey provides compounds that reduce inflammation in the brain, meaning it fights stress and anxiety.

- Drip cold water on your wrists. It cools arteries just under the skin which helps calm the whole body.

- Have sex. Sex is a sensory experience that helps us focus and release body tension. One Israeli study found that sex was a stress reliever (Journal of Social and Personal Relationships, Jan. 2012). Another study found that people who had sex had lower levels of cortisol (Psychosomatic Medicine, Oct. 2008).

- Reduce stress to reduce weight. Cortisol has been found to cause accumulation of abdominal fat as well as enlargement of fat cells (Chilnick, 2008).

- Add a desk plant. Humans have an innate need for nature. A desk plant creates separation from stressors and provides an opportunity for "soft fascination," giving yourself a chance to take a nature break and get away from work-related thoughts for a moment.

- Add an office pet. One study found that 90% of employees in pet-friendly workplaces feel highly connected to their company's mission and are fully engaged at work. In contrast, less than 65% of employees in non-pet workplaces made the same claims (Nationwide Pet Insurance).

- Meditate.

- Pray.

- Take up a craft that requires repetitive hand motions such as beading, knitting, clay modeling, chocolate making, woodworking.
- Try yoga.
- Smile. The facial muscles trigger endorphins.
- Watch a viral comedy video.
- Paint the walls.
- Plant flowers.
- Weed.
- Deadhead flowers.
- Create a Zen Zone in the debriefing room. Take 5 minutes of alone time to collect your thoughts and clear your head. Equip the room with aromatherapy, a heat wrap for your shoulders and neck, a tennis ball to massage the tension from your body, a stretch band to help you stretch sore muscles, fidget spinners and stress toys.
- Organize the clutter. It results in a sense of achievement that lifts your mood.
- Write a letter about your frustrations, then burn it (along with your frustration).
- Create a Personal Mission Statement to define yourself.
- Do a body scan.
    - Most of us ignore the signals our bodies are giving us throughout our day. This skill enables you to check in fairly quickly with your body to make adjustments or gather important information about your feelings.
    - To do a body scan, it is easiest to be sitting or laying down with eyes shut. Starting at the top of your head, notice the way your scalp and forehead feel. Then move down to notice your face, and so on. Mentally check in with each portion of your body.
    - If you come across an area that feels tense, simply linger there to take a relaxing breath, loosen the tension, and then continue on until you make it all the way down to your toes. This process can take as little or as long as you'd like.
- Reflect and problem solve. Break down what is causing the stress. Is it lack of time? Missing family time? Establishing the root of the stress can help you problem-solve how to relieve the strain, (National Health Service, 2020).
- Break down big projects. Create a checklist and break tasks down into less overwhelming goals. Keep things simple and focus on one task at a time, then cross it off. This strategy helps with energy conservation. The visual of your accomplishments will boost your focus. Also, double check to ensure that your workload is in line with your abilities and resources.

- Create an afterwork routine. Establish a routine to end your day to create a boundary between work and nonwork. Begin with quiet time as you drive home. Once home, try doing a crossword puzzle to give your brain a task to focus on. This will help you feel calmer and you'll be able to deal better with the stress.

- Do jumping jacks to get your heart rate up and activate your endorphins and cushion some of the anxiety.

- Binge-watch a good show. Instead of trying to contend with your ruminating or racing thoughts, get out of your head, place your attention elsewhere and transport you out of your life (positive distraction).

- Rub your feet over a golf ball for a relaxing massage.

- Avoid procrastination, which causes stress.

BALANCING EXERCISE: FROM DISTRESS TO EUSTRESS

- List one mini-escape or diversion that worked well to restore and renew you.
- List one thing that brings you joy.
- Name 3 things you feel grateful for today.
- Think of something that has brought you a sense of joy.
- Who do you love that you can reach out to today? Call them.
- What made you laugh today? Share it.

NOTES:

RESOURCES

ONLINE RESOURCES

ICARE™ LIBRARY

A comprehensive collection of over 150 topics, articles and evidence-based grief support resources available to your families 24/7. Seamless integration with your website.

$99 MONTHLY SUBSCRIPTION | ICARELIBRARY.COM

LITERATURE

RESILIENCE RX™ – ONE SHEETS

Resilience Rx™ one-sheets promotes nurturing evidence-based self-help techniques and positive coping strategies that support mourners through loss. Each Resilience Rx™ one sheet is a snapshot of an evidence-based healing modality and offers easy ways for how to implement it after loss. Use the one-sheets as office literature, at time of need packet, and as a mailing program for your families. Sold in packs of 10.

$15 PER SET | INTERNATIONALGRIEFINSTITUTE.COM/RESILIENCE

Sold in packs of 10. Size 8.5x11"

1. Chromotherapy
2. Dance/Movement Therapy
3. Forest Therapy
4. Hug Therapy
5. Laugh Therapy
6. Sensorial Therapy
7. Holiday Tips
8. Insomnia after loss
9. EMDR Therapy
10. Music Therapy
11. Knitting Therapy
12. Self-Care plan for the bereaved
13. Self-Care plan for widows

Books

GRIEF DIARIES AWARD-WINNING ANTHOLOGY SERIES
SEE ALL GRIEF DIARIES TITLES AT ALYBLUEMEDIA.COM

GRIEF DIARIES: SURVIVING LOSS OF A CHILD

Surviving Loss of a Child shares the poignant journeys of 22 women as they search for healing and hope after losing a child. Exploring how each mother faced a journey they couldn't fathom, **Surviving Loss of a Child** offers comfort and hope and is a reminder to others who find themselves facing the same journey that they can survive. Foreword by Grieving Men's R. Glenn Kelly.

$16.95 | ISBN: 978-1944328009
internationalgriefinstitute.com/product/100

GRIEF DIARIES: THROUGH THE EYES OF A WIDOW

Through the Eyes of a Widow is a collection of tender stories by widows as they learned to adapt after losing her husband. Each shares the challenges, where she found the most help, and the hope she found along the way.

$16.95 | ISBN: 978-1944328641
internationalgriefinstitute.com/product/101

GRIEF DIARIES: SURVIVING LOSS OF A SPOUSE

Surviving Loss of a Spouse features the poignant journeys of 15 men and women as they move through the aftermath of losing a husband or wife. Each narration offers a firsthand account of how each widow and widower faced the funeral, handled his or her spousal belongings, navigated the year of firsts, and how each fought to find hope in the aftermath. Foreword by award-winning playwright Carol Scibelli, author of Poor Widow Me.

$14.95 | ISBN: 978-1944328016
internationalgriefinstitute.com/product/104

GRIEF DIARIES: SURVIVING LOSS OF A PARENT

Whether one loses a parent in the natural order of life or it occurs much earlier than expected, the emotional aftermath can challenge our fears, familial relations, and even our sense of self. **Surviving Loss of a Parent** offers 17 firsthand accounts that yields a powerful look at how such losses can influence every aspect of our life. Foreword by radio host and author Christine Duminiak.

$14.95 | ISBN: 978-1944328078
internationalgriefinstitute.com/product/108

GRIEF DIARIES: SURVIVING LOSS OF A SIBLING

Losing a sibling is a heartbreak that leaves a hole in the fabric of every family. Facing a challenging journey that's often ignored cast into the shadows behind the bereaved parents, struggling through such emotions can be devastating lonely, **Surviving Loss of a Sibling** features the stories of 13 sisters and brothers as they fight to find the meaning of life without a sister or brother. Foreword by Benjamin Scott Allen.

$14.95 | ISBN: 978-1944328023
internationalgriefinstitute.com/product/106

GRIEF DIARIES: THROUGH THE EYES OF MEN

Breaking the man code and offering readers an inside look into the hidden world of male grief, Through the Eyes of Men features the stories of 14 men of different ages who tackle the tender subject of male bereavement from the very moment their lives changed with a loved one's death. Foreword by Glen Lord, past president of the national board of directors of The Compassionate Friends.

$15.95 | ISBN: 978-1944328481
internationalgriefinstitute.com/product/105

GRIEF DIARIES: SURVIVING LOSS BY SUICIDE

Three-time medalist, **Surviving Loss by Suicide** examines the aftermath of losing a loved one to suicide from the perspective of 12 different people. Voicing their thoughts and emotions through the funeral and beyond, each writer offers a candid look at a taboo journey. Foreword by award-winning author and suicide prevention advocate Emily Barnhardt.

$15.95 | ISBN: 978-1944328030

internationalgriefinstitute.com/product/102

GRIEF DIARIES: SURVIVING LOSS BY OVERDOSE

Book Excellence Awards Winner 2020, **Surviving Loss by Overdose** is a compilation of stories by 12 people who answered 18 questions about losing a loved one to overdose in hopes of raising awareness, educating, and inviting society to offer survivors the compassion that's often denied in a stigmatized death. Forward by Elaine M. Faulkner, SUDP.

$16.95 | ISBN: 978-1950712076

internationalgriefinstitute.com/product/103

GRIEF DIARIES: SURVIVING SUDDEN LOSS

Surviving Sudden Loss is a collection of 14 stories by parents, spouses, siblings, children, and grandparents who share their own personal insight into the hidden and often unspoken challenges of unexpectedly losing a loved one, including the emotional, mental, physical and social shifts they're forced to reckon with in the aftermath. With poignant narration, each writer shares the truth of their loss, where they found the most support, and how they rebuilt their lives in the aftermath. Coauthored by Maryann Mueller.

$18.95 | ISBN: 978-1944328894

internationalgriefinstitute.com/product/109

GRIEF DIARIES: SURVIVING LOSS BY CANCER

Surviving Loss by Cancer offers inspiring true stories about caring for a loved one with cancer all the way through to their final breath, and beyond. Filled with compassion and understanding, the collection of stories serve as a life raft in the storm of emotions, and offer readers hope, strength, courage after losing a loved one to cancer. Foreword by hospice director Dana Brothers.

$15.95 | ISBN: 978-1944328818
internationalgriefinstitute.com/product/110

GRIEF DIARIES: SURVIVING LOSS BY IMPAIRED DRIVING

A silver medalist in the 2016 USA Best Book Awards, **Loss by Impaired Driving** examines the journeys of 17 men and women who lost one or more loved ones to a drunk, drugged or impaired driver. A must read for young, new drivers and for AA groups. Foreword by Candace Lightner, founder of MADD.

$15.95 | ISBN: 978-1944328269
internationalgriefinstitute.com/product/112

GRIEF DIARIES: SURVIVING LOSS BY HOMICIDE

Surviving Loss by Homicide shares personal accounts of coping with a violent tragedy, and sheds insight into the strength needed to stay afloat in the aftermath of intense heartache and rollercoaster of emotions ranging from shock, anger, sadness and disbelief to healing and hope. Foreword by radio host Lady Justice.

$15.95 | ISBN: 978-1944328146
internationalgriefinstitute.com/product/113

ABOUT

She who heals others heals herself.
LYNDA CHELDELIN FELL

LYNDA CHELDELIN FELL is founder of the International Grief Institute, and international bestselling author of over 35 books including the award winning Grief Diaries series.

With her background as a firefighter/EMT, Lynda specializes in trauma, grief, compassion fatigue, and holds a national certification in critical incident stress management. A popular keynote speaker and educator, she is a member of the continuing education faculty at Whatcom Community College where she teaches classes on resilience, managing grief in the workplace, and compassion fatigue.

To research grief's impact on society, she has interviewed people around the world including societal figures such as Martin Luther King's daughter, and Heaven is For Real's Pastor Todd Burpo. She has earned six national literary awards and five national advocacy award nominations for her work.

lynda@internationalgriefinstitute.com

INVESTING IN COMMUNITY RESILIENCE

www.internationalgriefinstitute.com | 360-510-8590 | learn@internationalgriefinstitute.com